Contents

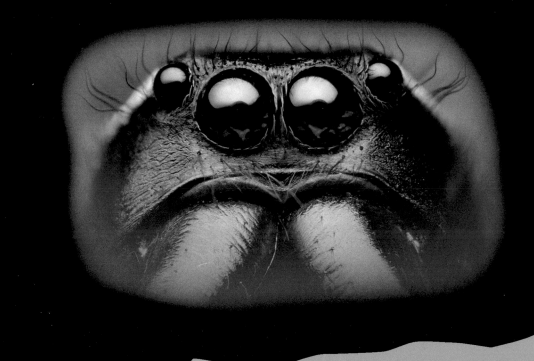

Monsters of the Deep

Since ancient times, sailors have told tales of huge, horrible sea monsters, often with big bulging eyes and terrifying tentacles. These monstrous animals were probably giant squid, which can grow to 13 metres long, with eyes the size of footballs.

◢ This squid is harmless, but some are fierce predators. A Humboldt squid has probing arms, tooth-lined tentacles, a raptor-like beak and a craving for flesh – even that of humans!

In September 2004, Japanese scientists Tsunemi Kubodera and Kyoichi Mori set out to be the first to photograph a live giant squid. They cast a line 900 metres down into the Pacific Ocean, baited with small squid and prawns. An automatic camera attached to the line was set to take a photo every 30 seconds.

Squid in the spotlight

As the scientists had hoped, a giant squid homed in on the bait. It grabbed the end of the line and got caught fast. The camera snapped a series of stunning photos before, four hours later, the squid got away.

In the struggle, the squid lost the end of one of its tentacles, which the team pulled aboard. It still worked, suckering itself onto the boat's deck and onto Kubodera's hands.

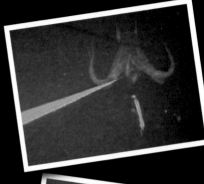

Giant squid have often been hunted by scientists and explorers. These images captured by Japanese scientists are from the first time a live giant squid has ever been photographed in the wild.

SQUID BRAINS

Squid are molluscs, like slugs and snails – but unlike snails, they are thought to be highly intelligent. They use colour changes to send messages, and some can use these signals to help them hunt together in packs.

Using the squid's severed tentacle as a guide, the scientists estimated that the creature must have been eight metres long.

Creepy-crawlies

There are thousands of species of insects and spiders, many of them unbelievably weird. How about a fly that invades an ant's body and turns it into a zombie, or spiders that can build a web bigger than your house?

▲ *Jumping spiders hop from place to place, dangling from a silk rope which they spin themselves. They are found in many countries around the world.*

Fire ants are a big problem in Texas and Florida in the USA. They bite people's legs, kill baby birds and even nibble through electrical cables. In 1997, American scientists came up with a solution – they introduced spooky phorid flies from South America. The flies don't simply attack the fire ants – they end up taking over their entire body from the inside!

Horrid phorids

First, the phorid fly females inject their eggs into the fire ants' bodies. The egg hatches into a maggot, which controls the ant's behaviour from inside its body, making it move away from the other fire ants. The maggot then eats the ant's brains, and its head falls off, forming a nest for the maggot. Finally the adult fly emerges from the ant's hollowed-out head about 40 days later.

⊘ *An adult phorid fly emerges from the dead ant's head.*

⬥ *A phorid fly homes in on an unsuspecting fire ant to lay an egg on it.*

⬥ *When it hatches, the maggot invades the fire ant's body. Eventually, the ant's head drops off.*

WORLD'S WIDEST WEB!

In 2007 the biggest spider web ever seen appeared in a park in Texas, USA. Experts think it was made by thousands of orb-weaver spiders working together. It covered several trees and a large area of ground, stretching a distance of more than 150 metres. The web started off white, but gradually turned brown as it had caught so many small flies.

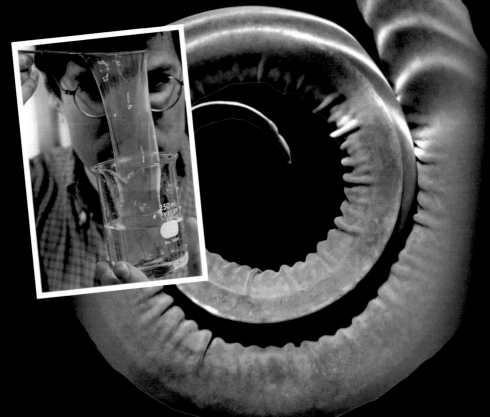

Slime Attack!

Slippery, gloopy slime is disgusting to most of us – but for a few weird creatures, it's just the stuff for getting out of a tight corner. In fact, some creatures are made of slime and not much else!

▶ *The hagfish is one of several creatures that use slime to ward off predators. An adult hagfish can produce enough slime to fill a small jug.*

Imagine trying to hold a smooth, snake-like fish in your hands. Before you can get a grip, you're covered in slime. This is the hagfish, one of the world's slimiest creatures. Scientists who study hagfish can't go near them without getting sticky slime all over them. It helps the hagfish to escape from all kinds of tricky situations.

One scientist even tasted the slime to see if it would put off a potential predator. Apparently it didn't have much taste at all – 'maybe a little bit salty'.

▼ *Slime moulds can grow up to several square metres in size and come in a variety of attractive shades, including yellow, brown and white. This variety is known as 'dog's vomit'.*

Hagfish habits

The weirdness doesn't stop there. Hagfish can tie a knot in themselves and slide it along their bodies, to push themselves out of another animal's grip. They have four hearts and two brains. They often burrow into living animals, and eat them from the inside out!

SLIME MOULDS

A slime mould looks like a lump of slimy jelly that appears overnight in woods or on lawns. People used to think these blobs came from space and named them 'star jelly'! But a slime mould is actually a colony, or group, of microscopic creatures that join together to form a super-blob that can crawl around.

Moles in Holes

Imagine spending your entire life in an underground tunnel and never seeing the light of day. If you were a naked mole rat, you'd have to – because the sun would blind your tiny eyes and burn your hairless skin.

▼ *A typical naked mole rat is about eight to ten centimetres long and uses its long sticking-out front teeth for digging.*

A bit like honey bees, naked mole rats from East Africa live in big groups, or colonies, with a queen to lead them. Only the queen has babies, and they all grow up to do useful jobs for the colony, such as digging new tunnels with their teeth or searching for tasty tubers (plant roots).

Hairless and blind

Naked mole rats have hardly any hair and are almost blind. To keep warm, they have to snuggle together in heaps or bask in parts of their burrow which are closer to the surface and heated by the sun.

But this strange life keeps them very safe from hunting animals, and some mole rats can live as long as 25 years. Recently, scientists have become very interested in mole rats because they never get cancer. Substances in their bodies might one day help us to beat the disease too.

FOLLOW YOUR NOSE!

The star-nosed mole of North America is probably the weirdest mole in the world. Its nose bristles with 22 tiny, touch-sensitive tentacles. This water-loving mole can hardly see, so it uses its nose to feel for insects, worms and water bugs to gobble up.

◀ Each of the star-nosed mole's nasal tentacles is covered with highly sensitive touch receptors that help it feel its way around.

Super-Squirters

If you're not careful, there are several strange creatures out there that will give you a good squirting. What do they squirt? Usually something revolting – like slime, blood or even vomit. Lovely!

▶ *Some horned lizards can squirt blood from the corners of their eyes to a distance of up to 1.5 metres.*

Blood squirts out here

When Spanish explorer Francisco Hernández travelled to Mexico in the 1500s, he was astonished to discover a bizarre spiky lizard which splattered him with a stream of blood from its eyes when he tried to touch it. This creature, the horned lizard, can build up the blood pressure in its head, until a weak spot next to its eye bursts, and a jet of blood shoots out.

Baby squirters

Several animals use squirting as a defence. One of the most disgusting is the baby fulmar, a common seabird. To avoid being attacked while its parents are out catching fish, it shoots disgusting, oily, fishy vomit out of its throat. Fulmar chicks have zapped several birdwatchers and wildlife experts right in the face. They can also squirt gloop at hunting birds, clogging up their feathers so they can't fly.

◀ *Don't get in the way of this fulmar chick – you could end up with an eyeful of vomit!*

DEADLY SQUIRTERS

Super-weird velvet worms that live in the Tropics use squirting power to catch food. They squirt glue at their prey, and it hardens into a sticky string that holds the victim fast. Then the worm slowly eats it up – and gobbles up its own slime too.

▲ *The velvet worm has glands on either side of its head which produce a sticky, milky-white slime to trap its prey.*

Wobbly but Deadly

What is a jellyfish? It's certainly not a fish, and it's much more than a jelly. These weird creatures, shaped like umbrellas with dangling tentacles, don't even have brains, yet they can be fierce hunters – and lethal to humans.

▼ *The highly poisonous lion's mane jellyfish is the largest in the world. It has been known to reach a width of 2.4 metres across.*

In 1997, Angel Yanagihara was swimming off the coast of Hawaii when she was stung by a swarm of box jellyfish. These are among the most dangerous creatures in the world. Their tentacles, which can reach three metres long, inject a painful venom that affects the body's muscles and nerves. When Yanagihara was stung, she was soon struggling to breathe and had to be resuscitated by doctors.

Lucky escape

Yanagihara was lucky. She made a full recovery and went on to devote her life to jellyfish research. Many others have not been so fortunate. Box jellyfish have killed dozens of people in the seas around Australia and South-East Asia.

▶ *A Hawaiian lifeguard holds up two box jellyfish found on Waikiki Beach. The poison dripping from the tentacles can still be dangerous even after the jellyfish is dead.*

JELLYFISH ALERT!

The Australian box jellyfish is one of the most venomous of all sea creatures. Pain from the sting is so intense that victims go into immediate shock and rarely make it back to shore on their own. Contact with the tentacles can cause heart failure within minutes and is nearly always fatal.

Masters of Disguise

Now you see them, now you don't!
Some creatures are so brilliant
at disguising themselves to blend
in with their surroundings,
you'd hardly know they're
there at all!

▼ The amazing geometer moth can make itself almost invisible against the bark of this tree in South Texas, USA.

The mimic octopus can adopt a whole range of different disguises to ward off attackers. Here it copies the shape and colours of a starfish.

In 1998, scientists diving off the coast of Indonesia in South-East Asia came across a bizarre octopus that they had never seen before. As it searched the flat, sandy seabed for food, the creature, named the mimic octopus, hid from hungry predators by imitating a range of other, more dangerous animals.

Sea snake

To copy a deadly sea snake, the octopus stuffed its body into a hole in the sand, sticking out two of its legs in a long snake shape. It also changed its shape and colour to mimic jellyfish or stingrays. It was even able to use its abilities for hunting – for example imitating a crab to attract other crabs, then snapping them up!

Shape and texture

Unlike chameleons, which can only change colour, mimic octopuses can copy as many as 15 other species. As well as disguising their shape, they can also change their texture to match rocks, seaweed or coral.

This Peruvian katydid or bush-cricket keeps out of trouble by disguising itself as a leaf.

LEAVES, PEBBLES AND POOS

Many creatures hide from their enemies by looking like objects around them. Leaf insects and stick insects look just like parts of plants, and pebble plants look like stones – while the tiger swallowtail caterpillar does a good impression of a bird dropping!

Pesky Parasites

A parasite is a creature that lives in or on another creature. Parasites are found throughout nature, and humans are no strangers to them – we have lots of creepy creatures sharing our bodies!

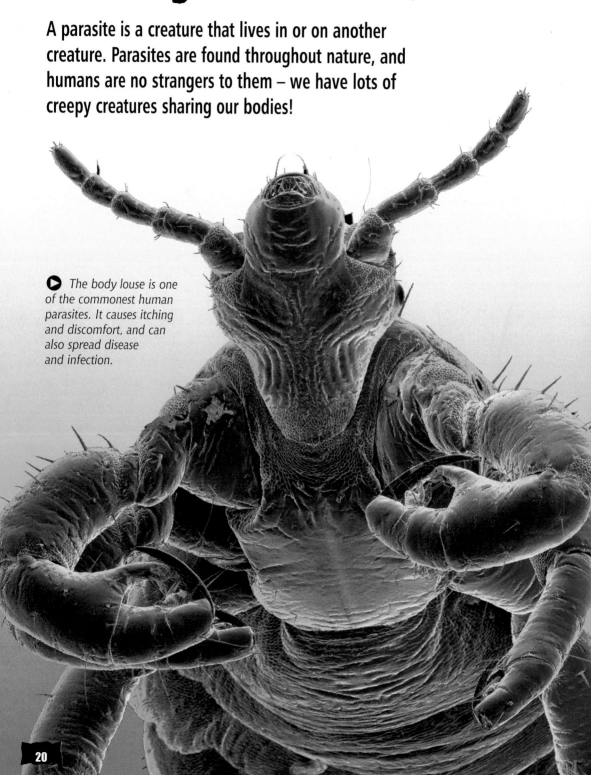

▶ *The body louse is one of the commonest human parasites. It causes itching and discomfort, and can also spread disease and infection.*

Luckily, the parasites on us aren't as weird – or as big – as the peculiar tongue-eating louse. In 2005, a shopper in London bought a snapper fish. While preparing to cook it, they found a bizarre bug-like creature filling the fish's mouth. It was a tongue-eating louse (actually a type of crustacean).

A new tongue

In its natural home in the Pacific Ocean, the louse attaches itself to the snapper's tongue, then sucks all the blood out of it until it falls off.

Even weirder, the louse then stays inside the snapper's mouth, feeding on its blood and acting as a replacement tongue! The snapper can wiggle it around and use it in just the same way as the original tongue.

⚠ The tongue-eating louse ceratothoa imbricata in the mouth of a South African black tail (diplodus capensis). After eating the tongue of its host, the louse attaches itself to the muscles at the base of the tongue stub.

BUGS ON YOU

There are thousands of parasites living and feeding on our bodies. Most are so tiny we don't even notice them. Some of the bacteria in our intestines are vital for protecting us against infection. Others are less useful – like the little mites that hang around us to feed on flakes of our dead skin. Most people have eyelash mites – tiny wriggly creatures that live around the roots of eyelashes!

⚠ A hugely magnified view of an eyelash mite.

Bird-brained Boogies

Some male birds do such crazy dances when they're trying to impress a mate, you can hardly even tell what kind of animals they are. Others look so silly, it's amazing they ever get a girlfriend.

▽ To wow a female, the male blue-footed booby does a curious dance that involves spreading his wings and waving each of his big, flappy feet in turn. Luckily for him, she usually likes it – though our name for this bird, booby, comes from the Spanish for 'clown' or 'idiot'.

Colourful courtship

Few courtship displays are more colourful than those of the male birds of paradise of New Guinea. Each species has its own spectacular shapes, colours and dances. Females watch up to 20 different males displaying, before finally choosing a partner.

⬤ *A male Raggiana bird of paradise displays his splendid tail feathers in the jungle of Papua New Guinea.*

A superb performance

The species known as the superb bird of paradise has one of the world's most famous mating dances. First, the male bird clears a space and rubs it clean with leaves. Then he spreads out a fan of black feathers behind his head, along with brilliant blue feathers from his chest, to make a wide oval shape. With the two blue spots on his head, it looks like a strange alien face. In this position, he hops up and down making a clicking sound.

◀ *The male imperial shag bends over backwards to impress his mate.*

Hammerhead Hunters

Sharks are among the ocean's deadliest predators. You may think of them as fast, fierce and scary, but some are extraordinarily peculiar too.

◆ Scientists believe that the weirdly shaped head of the hammerhead shark helps it to hunt for food, by allowing it to see through 360 degrees.

◀ The huge nose of the goblin shark contains special sensors that help it to detect its prey. Once within range, it sticks out its jaws and uses a tongue-like muscle to suck the victim towards its razor-sharp teeth.

The hammerhead shark has one of the weirdest heads of any animal, but that doesn't stop it from being a hungry hunter – and a deadly predator. In one famous case, three hammerheads were caught off Long Island in America in 1805. Inside one of them were the remains of a man's body, chomped into pieces, along with the shreds of his stripy shirt.

Feared by pirates

Hammerheads were always feared by pirates and have recently been blamed for several deadly attacks. As their eyes are on the sides of their wide hammer-shaped heads, they can see all around them as well as straight ahead. They also have highly sensitive organs for picking up electrical signals from their prey, and are said to collect in big shoals around sinking ships to look for bodies in the water.

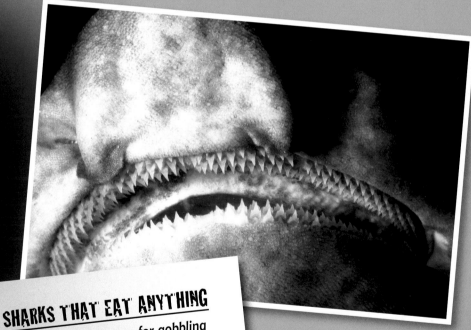

SHARKS THAT EAT ANYTHING

Tiger sharks are known for gobbling up all kinds of rubbish along with their prey. Weird things found inside the stomachs of dead tiger sharks include plastic bags, shoes and pyjamas, tin cans and glass bottles, a human arm, linoleum, chicken wire and bits of crocodiles. No wonder tiger sharks are called the 'dustbins of the sea'.

⬥ Tiger sharks' teeth are specially adapted for slicing through tough materials like bone and turtleshell. As they wear out, new rows constantly move forward to replace them.

The Weird Awards

Which creature is the weirdest of them all?
Take a look at these weird record-breakers.

▼ *This nocturnal creature known as the aye-aye lives in the forests of Madagascar. It has rodent-like teeth and a long, thin middle finger which it uses to pick out grubs from the bark of trees.*

SLIMIEST

Scientists often say the hagfish is the slimiest creature in the sea. But the world record for slimiest creature has to go to the slime mould, which is made of pure slime.

MOST LUMINOUS

The most luminous creature is probably the deep-sea flashlight fish. The two bright flashing lamps on its head are so bright that people have mistaken them for divers with underwater torches.

LOUDEST

The pistol shrimp and the blue whale compete for the title of loudest creature. The whale's song and the shrimp's snapping claws have both been measured at around 190 decibels – louder than a jet plane taking off.

MOST POISONOUS

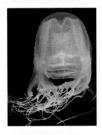

The box jellyfish is thought to produce the most powerful poison of any animal. But the deadliest poison of all is probably made by clostridium botulinum, a type of bacteria found in soil.

MOST LEGGY

The name 'millipede' means 'a thousand legs', but no millipede actually has this many. The record-holder is the rare Illacme plenipes millipede of North America, with up to 750 legs.

LONGEST-LIVING

Sea sponges live on the ocean bed and draw food and oxygen from the water. One type found in the Antarctic is thought to be able to live for 1,500 years or more.

Weird Creature Finder

How likely are you to come across one of the weird creatures in this book? It depends where you live (or where you go on holiday). Use this guide to check out where each bizarre beast can be found.

Name	Where found
Blue-footed booby	Islands and coasts of the eastern Pacific Ocean
Blue whale	Mainly far northern and southern oceans
Box jellyfish	Seas around South-East Asia and Australia
Clostridium botulinum	Widespread around the world
Eyelash mites	Worldwide, wherever humans live
Fire ant	Worldwide, except very cold areas
Flashlight fish	Tropical seas and oceans
Fulmar	Far northern and southern oceans
Giant squid	Deep oceans around the world
Hagfish	Seas and oceans worldwide
Hammerhead shark	Tropical and temperate (warm) seas and oceans
Horned lizard	North and Central America
Illacme plenipes millipede	California, USA
Leaf insect	Australia and southern Asia
Mimic octopus	Seas around Indonesia
Naked mole rat	Eastern Africa
Orb-weaver spider	Many species found worldwide
Pebble plant	Dry areas in southern Africa
Phorid fly	Worldwide, especially in warm areas
Pistol shrimp	Seas and oceans worldwide
Slime mould	Worldwide
Star-nosed mole	North America
Stick insect	Widespread around the world
Superb bird of paradise	New Guinea, an island in South-East Asia
Tiger shark	Tropical seas and oceans around the world
Tiger swallowtail caterpillar	North America
Tongue-eating louse	Pacific Ocean
Velvet worm	Southern tropical areas

Glossary

bacteria very small living things that can sometimes cause diseases

bait food put down to trap an animal

biologist someone who studies living things

cancer a disease that makes body cells grow out of control

colony a group of creatures of the same species that live together and help each other

coral sea creature which forms a hard, stone-like outer skeleton

courtship behaviour of an animal to attract a mate

crustacean a type of animal with a hard shell, such as a crab or shrimp

decibel a measure of volume of sound

gland a part of the body that produces a chemical substance

host the body which a parasite lives on

linoleum a type of floor covering

maggot a baby fly with a worm-like shape

marine to do with the sea

mate to get together with a partner to have babies

microscopic too small to be seen without a microscope

mimic to copy or imitate

mite a type of tiny spider-like creature

mollusc a soft-bodied creature, such as a slug or snail

nocturnal active at night

octopus a sea creature with eight **tentacles**

parasite a creature that lives in or on another living thing

predator a creature that attacks and eats other living things

raptor a bird of prey

receptor an organ that responds to an outside stimulus

resuscitate to revive or bring back to life

rodent a mammal with strong teeth for gnawing

shoal a large group of fish or sea creatures

species a particular type of living thing

tentacle a long, flexible arm-like part of an animal

toxin a poison

tuber a root-like part of a plant that grows underground

venom a poison used by a creature to hurt its enemies or prey

zombie in stories, someone who is dead but can still walk around

Websites

www.animalplanet.ca/galleryList.aspx?sid=18261
TV presenter Nick Baker's weird creatures gallery.

www.factmonster.com/spot/unusualanimals1.html
Interesting facts about bizarre and unusual creatures.

www.newscientist.com/gallery/new-species
Bizarre animals that are new to science.

Note to parents and teachers:

Every effort has been made by the Publishers to ensure that the websites in this book are suitable for children, that they are of the highest educational value, and that they contain no inappropriate or offensive material. However, because of the nature of the Internet, it is impossible to guarantee that the contents of these sites will not be altered. We strongly advise that Internet access is supervised by a responsible adult.

Index